Whispers of Inspirations

for

Busy Women

One Minute Inspirations to Refresh

Your Mind, Body and Spirit

Sandy Philbin

DEDICATION

This book is dedicated first and foremost to God who placed these inspirations in my heart. To my husband, Barry, who believes in me and encourages me to keep following my dreams. To my mom, my inspiration of unconditional love, who is always close to my heart and left this earth much too early at forty-nine years of age. To my dad who was an incredible entrepreneur and unknowingly inspired me to follow in his footsteps. To my two brothers, Stan and Tom, who continually share their love and encouragement. To all other family members and heart friends too numerous to mention here who continue to travel with me along this journey of life. Thank you all for your love and friendship.

May these inspirations bless you as you have all blessed me.

Blessings and Love from My Heart to Yours,
Sandy

Dear Maria,
May your heart
be touched by
inspiration.
Love & Blessings,
Sandy
Jeremiah 29:11

2020

CONTENTS - INSPIRATIONS BY NUMBER

ACKNOWLEDGMENTS

This book was inspired by God and the quiet whispers He placed in my heart. He brought people and situations into my life during a time when I felt lost and purposeless. He led me down the path to write this book on inspirations for women who may have the same feelings at times and who long to slow down and live a more peaceful, abundant, fulfilling and purposeful life. There are times when I have entered the desert for extended periods of time while writing this book. It has been a slow process with many challenges along the way. By God's grace, I was blessed to finish this book and share what I have learned from life with you. To God be the glory!

There are so many people who have supported and encouraged me through this journey and brought this book to fruition. My husband Barry Philbin, my forever love, whose kind and loving heart encourages me to believe in myself and never quit. Stan, Tom and Nancy who all listen patiently when I talk on and on and other family members and heart friends who encourage me with their love and kind words. I will always hold each of you forever within my heart. A heartfelt thank you to Janet, Pat, Kelly, Kathy, Ann, Val, Diane, Steph, Melissa and Sue for their encouraging words and feedback along this journey.

My work has also been greatly inspired first and foremost by God through the Holy Spirit. Also, the writings and teachings of so many others have inspired me throughout my life it is hard to capture them all. Here is a list of a few people in alphabetical order who greatly impacted and blessed my life: Donald Altman, Danna Beal, Joan Z. Borysenko, Katie Brazelton, Richard and Kimmy Brooke, Brendon Burchard, Maria Andros Buckley, Rhonda Byrne, Jack Canfield, Kristine Carlson, Minnie Claiborne, Paul Chek, Penny Cosner, Sue Eller, Karen Ely, Debbie Ford, Holley Gerth, Elizabeth George, Pat Gillis, Anne Louise

Gittleman, Billy Graham, Louis L. Hay, Sarah Harnish, Esther Hicks, Karen L. Hopkins, Chip Ingram, Dr. David Jeremiah, Jackie M. Johnson, Sue Johnson, Loral Langemeier, Joni Lamb, Sage Lavine, Mona Lisa, Max Lucado, Therese Marszalek, John Maxwell, Joyce Meyers, Carolyn Myss, Stormie Omartian, Joel Osteen, Cheryl Richardson, Deni Robinson, Jacob Roig, J.P. Sears, Teri Secrest, Anne Wilson Schaef, Renee Swope, Madisyn Taylor, Lysa TerKeurst, Women of Faith Team, D. Gary and Mary Young, and Jon Kabit-Zin.

There are many more too numerous to mention here, who inspire me every day. A heartfelt thank you to all for sharing your wisdom and life journey with the world. If there is anyone I unknowingly have not acknowledged, please accept my sincere apologies. I will make any corrections or additions in future editions of this book.

WELCOME TO

Whispers of Inspirations
for
Busy Women
One Minute Inspirations to Refresh Your Mind, Body and Spirit

There are many inspirational books written every year, and each book you read fulfills a specific purpose at a specific time in your life. Today, I believe you have been led to choose my book for reasons yet to be revealed. May your heart be filled with joy and your spirit refreshed as you read these 52 one-minute inspirations. So many women I meet are challenged with balancing their lives between family, work, volunteering, church, etc., resulting in anxiety, frustration, burnout, and feelings of being overwhelmed. Their days seem to get shorter as their lists get longer. Time for self-care seems to be non-existent and a pure impossibility. Many women long for time to relax and de-stress yet, never schedule the time to do so. Is this you? Can you relate? Believe me, I am walking right by your side because I experience these same challenges. I tend to put others first, neglecting my own needs to relax and restore. Once I realized I am the only one who can create and control my life and choices, I *chose* to overcome my feelings of guilt for taking care of myself and began to practice loving myself enough to practice self-care each day even if only for one minute. Remember, you are a human being, not a human doing - a spiritual being having a physical experience. God did not put you on earth to complete your "to do" list. You are here to fulfill HIS plan for your life. Let's walk along this journey of life together.

Over the years I have learned and continue to learn about the importance of self-love and self-care. It is not a selfish act to take care of yourself, so please do not feel guilty when you begin to pamper yourself. It is so important to spend time on self-care for your mind, body and spirit to restore and heal. How will you stay healthy and balanced to fulfill the purpose of your life or help others if you do not plan time to nurture yourself? My heart's desire is for these heart-centered whispers of inspirations to be a catalyst of change for you as you begin and continue your journey to self-care and self-love. Make a promise to yourself today to schedule time every day for YOU before someone else does. These inspirations are a great place to begin. Take one minute each week to read and reflect on an inspiration. Allow your heart to guide you to inspiration as you begin your new journey to take care of YOU. You are worthy of this minute for self-care and self-love. Congratulations on taking the first step of your journey.

Even though this book is written from a woman's perspective, I invite anyone to read these inspirations of encouraging words and thoughts for reflection and who has a willingness to experience a new journey of life.

How to Use This Book

There are 52 weekly inspirations. Each inspiration is numbered. Let your heart guide you to inspiration. You may be led to read each inspiration consecutively, or your heart may guide you to the inspiration that is perfect for you at that moment. Certain inspirations may resonate more than others with your inner soul depending on where you are in your life journey. Re-read and meditate on the inspirations to allow the whispers to speak to your heart as they guide you to messages of wisdom you are seeking. Some inspirations will encourage you, and some will be challenging. Some inspirations will take you to a place of relief and comfort which we all seek. While reading an inspiration, open your heart without judgment or expectations and be willing to receive the message. A certain inspiration may reveal an area in your life needing attention or focus. Allow whatever happens to happen. You are right where you are meant to be at this moment, and all is well. There is a blank page after each inspiration to journal your thoughts.

Before reading an inspiration, focus on the present moment and open your heart to receive what is revealed. Then, take three deep diaphragmatic breaths to center your mind, calm your soul and prepare your heart. A diaphragmatic breath comes from deep within your lungs and the inner core of your being. Place both hands on your ribcage with your palms facing your body and your fingers loosely interlaced. As you take a deep breath from your diaphragm, your fingers will move slightly apart as your lungs fill with oxygen and will come back together as you exhale. You will begin to feel the rise and fall of your ribcage as you breathe diaphragmatically. It is important to keep your chest relaxed to prevent shallow breathing. If your mind begins to wander, acknowledge your thoughts that arise, then gently bring your attention back to your breath.

After reading an inspiration, take a minute to journal your thoughts and set your intention based on the message you receive. Then, write three Whispers of Gratitude in this book or in your journal that speak to your heart. Expressing gratitude heals and balances your emotions, lifts your spirits and fills your heart with love to share with others.

Enhance your experience while reading an inspiration with calming music, aromatherapy and essential oils for emotional balancing, spiritual awareness and inspiration. For example, choose your favorite essential oil before reading each inspiration. A*lways* read instructions before use. My personal knowledge about essential oils is based upon experience with Young Living Essential Oils. To *diffuse*, follow the instructions with your diffuser. To *inhale*, place one or two drops of oil in the palm of your hand. Then, using the other hand, rub the oil into the palm of your hand three times in a clockwise motion to activate the oil. Place the palm of your hand gently by your nose and inhale the fragrance of the oil while reading the inspiration. Take a few minutes to allow the words to penetrate deep into your heart to restore and heal your mind, body and spirit. For a deeper experience while reading an inspiration, create a quiet, sacred place that includes personal and sentimental items.

If this book touches your heart and blesses you, share your love and blessings with your heart friends. Encourage them to let their light shine brightly and illuminate the world with joy, peace, kindness and the power of love by sharing this book with them. I would love to hear which inspiration(s) touched your heart. I invite you to visit sandyphilbin.com or @sandyphilbin for more heart-centered information.

Blessings and Love from my Heart to Yours,
Sandy

1 EMOTIONAL BALANCING

Faith, Feelings and Emotions

Do you have days when nothing goes as planned? Does this change your emotions and feelings? Do you begin to lose faith and feel discouraged or frustrated and out of balance? Emotions affect feelings. Some days you may experience feelings of love and joy and other days you may have feelings of anger or hopelessness. When you experience the latter, this may be an opportunity to practice living your life by faith versus feelings and to balance your emotions. To become emotionally balanced, begin to align your thoughts, feelings, emotions and actions with what you would like to see manifest in your life. Remember to nurture yourself when you feel weak as well as when you feel strong.

Take three deep diaphragmatic breaths and ask God to reveal imbalances in your life so you may begin to balance your emotions. Listen and trust God to guide you according to His plans for the day then, take a step of faith.

Journal your thoughts about ways you can begin to live your life by faith. As you begin to walk by faith, you will notice a calming and uplifting feeling as you let go and let God bring your emotions back into balance.

Whispers of Gratitude...What three things are you grateful for today?

_____

_____

_____

Blessings and Love from my Heart to Yours,
Sandy

2 ENLIGHTENED AWARENESS

Slow Down

Is your day filled up with a bunch of "to do" lists and requests from others, causing you to lose sight of and miss experiencing time for tranquility and restoration? Awareness is the first step to restoration. Practice enlightened awareness by blocking out time for yourself each day. Make a commitment to yourself to keep this appointment for meditation, prayer or mindful breathing. Or, schedule time for a short mindful meditation walk allowing the healing and majestic powers of nature to refresh your spirit.

Take three deep diaphragmatic breaths whenever you feel like you are running around in circles with no time to slow down. Breathe mindfully following each inhalation and exhalation from beginning to end to stay in the present moment.

Journal one step you will take today to slow down, become aware of your surroundings and practice enlightened awareness.

Whispers of Gratitude...What three things are you grateful for today?

_____

_____

_____

Blessings and Love from my Heart to Yours,
Sandy

3 LOVE AND GRACE

Choose to Love

Love is both a choice and an act of the will. Sometimes it may be difficult to extend love to others especially if we have been hurt. It is during these times when God's grace is necessary to extend love to the unlovable especially when we do not "feel like" being loving. When we choose to love with little acts of kindness, words of encouragement, a hug or a prayer, our feelings begin to change because our heart begins to change.

Take three deep diaphragmatic breaths and a minute to pray and reflect on what you can do to choose and extend love to the unlovable and ways to re-energize your love. Then, watch your love blossom and grow by the grace of God.

Journal about a time when God extended His love and grace to you or someone you did not feel like extending love to. What did you experience?

Whispers of Gratitude...What three things are you grateful for today?

_____

_____

_____

Blessings and Love from my Heart to Yours,

Sandy

4 THE HEART OF FRIENDSHIP

Promptings Within Your Heart

Friendship is reaching out for someone's hand and touching their heart. Do you have days when someone is continually on your mind and in your heart? These thoughts may be the quiet whispers of your heart prompting you to reach out to this person by phone, email, text or a card in the mail to let them know you are thinking of them. I believe we are all spiritually connected because we are made from God's love and in His image. Our spirit is always active and may prompt us when we are called to do something for another. You may be the answer to someone's prayer by lifting their spirit and bringing joy to their day.

Take three deep diaphragmatic breaths and be open to the thoughts you have about another. The first person who comes to your mind is a prompt from within your heart letting you know this may be the one you are meant to reach out to today. Reach out now and be a blessing to them.

Journal about the promptings within your heart and who you may need to reach out to today.

Whispers of Gratitude...What three things are you grateful for today?

_____

_____

_____

Blessings and Love from my Heart to Yours,

Sandy

5 WHISPERS OF SPRING

A Time of Renewal and Growth

Take a moment to imagine living your dream life. Maybe you envision having a dream home, a peaceful marriage, time for travel, financial freedom or a flourishing business.

Spring is the perfect time of year for new beginnings, change and transformation. The gentle sounds of nature come alive. Flowers begin to blossom from the nourishment of the sun and the earth, preparing to fulfill their purpose. Spring is a time of renewal and growth. Is there something you would like to change or do in your life which may require you to step outside of your comfort zone and to be strong, courageous and fearless?

Take three deep diaphragmatic breaths. Then, let the quiet whispers of your heart guide you as you reflect on this time of renewal and growth.

Journal any thoughts that arise. Then, pray for God to guide and prepare you for the transformation and new beginnings.

Whispers of Gratitude...What three things are you grateful for today?

_____

_____

_____

Blessings and Love from my Heart to Yours,

Sandy

6 OVERCOMING PERFECTIONISM

When Good Enough Is Good Enough

Perfectionism can keep you from living a fulfilling and purposeful life by causing anxiety, self-doubt or self-sabotaging behaviors. Perfectionism is part of your ego setting you up for failure before you even take the first step. You may compare yourself to others and belittle what you do through procrastination or you may be unable to make decisions. What you do never seems to be good enough in your own eyes, destroying your confidence and creativity. Perfectionism will stop you from moving forward by causing feelings of failure and self-doubt, creating a vicious cycle of self-sabotaging behaviors. The next time you notice yourself being a perfectionist, remind yourself that good enough is good enough. Expecting perfectionism all the time will keep you from living a joyful and fulfilling life and may lead to more sabotaging behaviors.

Take three deep diaphragmatic breaths whenever you move into your perfectionistic mindset and remind yourself, today you will do your very best and then let God take care of all the rest.

Journal one or two ways you can overcome perfectionism when it arises freeing you to live a joyful life.

Whispers of Gratitude...What three things are you grateful for today?

_____

_____

_____

Blessings and Love from my Heart to Yours,

Sandy

7 THE JOURNEY TO YOUR DREAMS

Opportunities Along the Way

The anticipation and journey towards a goal or a dream can sometimes be more exciting than reaching your destination. Life teaches you what you need to learn along the journey to your dreams. There will be days when you take two steps forward and three steps back leading you to do a course correction in your life. This may cause you to focus on the obstacles and challenges along the way, resulting in discouragement and disbelief. Remember, God placed this dream in your heart and wants to give you the desires of your heart. As of today, begin to look at each obstacle or challenge as an opportunity to keep you moving forward towards your goals and dreams.

Take three deep diaphragmatic breaths to calm your mind and center your thoughts as you meditate on God's word. Reflect upon the opportunities that brought you closer to your dreams.

Journal your thoughts about times when an obstacle you faced became an opportunity turning your dream into a reality.

Whispers of Gratitude...What three things are you grateful for today?

_____

_____

_____

Blessings and Love from my Heart to Yours,

Sandy

8 YOUR GREATEST TEACHER

Daily Lessons

Each day you are given the opportunity to learn and grow from your greatest teacher... LIFE! When you were born, your life did not come with a step by step instruction book on how to live each day. People and situations will teach you what you are meant to learn along the way such as patience, love, forgiveness, compassion, trust, faith and more. The next time you need some guidance about the next step to take in your life, find a quiet place or go to your sacred space to calm your mind and be alone to listen to the quiet whispers within your heart.

Take three deep diaphragmatic breaths, then pray and ask God for wisdom to become aware of the lesson life is presenting to you. Pray for the willingness to open your heart and accept and understand these lessons for you are right where you are meant to be at this given moment.

Journal your insights and the whispers of your heart about what life may be teaching you for the day. Continue to journal your thoughts so you can go back for reflection and be reminded of the lesson(s) you learned.

Whispers of Gratitude...What three things are you grateful for today?

_____

_____

_____

Blessings and Love from my Heart to Yours,

Sandy

9 YOUR PHYSICAL BEING

How Are You Treating Your Temple?

Your physical body is a temple and gift from your Creator and is needed on earth to fulfill your divine purpose. Therefore, it is important to practice self-care and self-love to keep your physical temple healthy. If you avoid paying attention to your physical health, it can affect your emotional health resulting in an imbalance preventing you from living your life to the fullest and carrying out your purpose. How are you treating your temple? Do you practice mindful breathing, eat nourishing foods, exercise, meditate, pray and take time each day for rest and relaxation? It is important to focus on each of these areas to maintain physical and emotional balance.

Take three deep diaphragmatic breaths and reflect on which area needs more of your attention.

Journal one small step you can take today to practice self-care and self-love to nurture your physical temple, the vehicle to fulfill your life's purpose.

Whispers of Gratitude...What three things are you grateful for today?

_____

_____

_____

Blessings and Love from my Heart to Yours,

Sandy

10 DECISIONS, DECISIONS, DECISIONS

Inner Purpose

We are all faced with decisions each day and may wonder if we made the right decision. Whether a decision is right or wrong is based on perception. There are no perfect decisions. We live in a world which revolves around doing vs. being focused on the external world vs. our inner being. When you are faced with a decision, begin to focus on your inner purpose which is *being* instead of your outer purpose which is *doing*. You were created as a human "being" not a human doing. As you learn the difference between being and doing, the right decision will be waiting for you along with the blessings. It is all a part of your spiritual journey on earth. Sometimes you may lose sight of the blessings in your decisions. However, blessings are always there regardless of what decision you make.

Take three deep diaphragmatic breaths when you are faced with a decision. Then, believe and trust God to guide you. He will always lead you to the outcome that is best for you and according to His plan no matter what decision you make.

Take one minute to journal about a decision you need to make. Listen to your heart and make note of any thoughts that enter your mind. Once you make the decision, believe, trust and never look back.

Whispers of Gratitude...What three things are you grateful for today?

_____

_____

_____

Blessings and Love from my Heart to Yours,

Sandy

11 PERFECT TIMING

The Right Place at the Right Time

Our lives are perfectly timed by God. Wherever you are at this moment is exactly where you are meant to be. This moment is the only moment you truly have. Whatever is happening in your life right now has a purpose and might be divinely orchestrated for you at this specific time. A person may come into your life to guide you to the next path along your journey of life, encourage you, provide emotional support and love or teach you something you are ready to learn at the given moment. There is a time and a purpose for everything in our lives.

Take three deep diaphragmatic breaths as you listen to the quiet whispers of your heart for guidance while becoming aware of the here and now without thinking of the past or the future. Be assured you are right where you need to be and will always be in the right place at the right time.

Journal your thoughts and reflect upon where your life is right now and trust you are exactly where you need to be at this moment in time.

Whispers of Gratitude...What three things are you grateful for today?

_____

_____

_____

Blessings and Love from my Heart to Yours,

Sandy

12   SEND LOVE TO OTHERS

Become a Beacon of Light and Love

You are a creation of light and love. Love is the greatest power and highest frequency in the world. Choose today to be a beacon of light and love and send love to others. Always remember, you are a divine creation, created from love. You are loved and have been created from love. Take a deep breath, then, imagine a majestic light of love surrounding you and being absorbed deep within your heart. Set your intention today to send this love to others and open your heart to receive this love back from the world.

Take three more deep diaphragmatic breaths and notice if a specific person enters your mind? This may be the person who needs to feel your light and love at this very moment!

Journal your thoughts about how you can be a beacon of light and love for this person or other people who come to mind or cross your path each day.

Whispers of Gratitude...What three things are you grateful for today?

_____

_____

_____

Blessings and Love from my Heart to Yours,
Sandy

13 HIDDEN BLESSINGS

Retrain Your Mind

When we focus on what we do not have we may miss the blessings in our life. Even through times of adversity, there are hidden blessings. For instance, a disagreement or an argument with a loved one or friend may be necessary for the growth of your character, teaching you to overcome the need to control others or allowing others to express their point of view. We tend to focus on the negative outcome of circumstances due to past conditioning. Begin today to retrain your mind and look for the blessings rather than focusing on the downside.

Take three deep diaphragmatic breaths and a minute to reflect upon three things you have in your life, something you have done or something someone else has done for you that blessed you.

Journal about the blessings you received throughout your life as a reminder to retrain your mind and become aware of hidden blessings. As you begin to retrain your mind your view of life will begin to change.

Whispers of Gratitude...What three things are you grateful for today?

_____

_____

_____

Blessings and Love from my Heart to Yours,

Sandy

14 CREATE A CALMING OASIS

Nature's Gifts

Life can present unexpected challenges and stressful situations. We are blessed with gifts of nature to help us through these times. Whenever you are faced with a difficult situation or feeling stressed and out of balance, spend time out in nature. A mindful, meditative walk in nature while focusing on each step you take helps to relieve stress and quiet your thoughts. Creation has provided us with plants, trees, shrubs, flowers and fruit. Their natural oils help to maintain our health and emotional balance. Experience nature's gifts with these essential oils. Create your very own personal calming oasis to refresh your mind, body and spirit by placing 1-2 drops of your favorite essential oil in the palms of one hand, rub clockwise with the other hand three times then, inhale the aroma to relax and lift your mood. Ahhhh...feel the calm.

Take three deep diaphragmatic breaths throughout the day to center and relax your mind and body. Whenever possible, step out into nature to refresh your spirit.

Journal your thoughts about different ways nature's gifts help you to create your calming oasis.

Whispers of Gratitude...What three things are you grateful for today?

_____

_____

_____

Blessings and Love from my Heart to Yours,
Sandy

15 HEART FRIENDS

Friends Who Love from the Heart

There are various forms of friendships, and each one brings a special joy and blessing to our lives. We have acquaintances, casual friends, close friends and "heart friends." A heart friend is a friend who loves from the heart and is a friend who you trust to share your deepest feelings, fears and desires with. A heart friend is a person who encourages, listens and supports you during good times or bad, a friend who wants the best for you and loves and accepts you for who you are.

Take three deep diaphragmatic breaths and reflect upon someone who is your heart friend. Express gratitude for your heart friend who blesses and brings joy to your life. Send them love and a "thinking of you" message virtually or through a handwritten notecard. You may be the light that brightens a gloomy day.

Reflect upon and journal your thoughts about your experiences and the many blessings you have experienced with your heart friends.

Whispers of Gratitude...What three things are you grateful for today?

_____

_____

_____

Blessings and Love from my Heart to Yours,
Sandy

16 LET YOUR LIGHT SHINE

Illuminate the World

God has given each one of us special gifts and talents to share with others. Your light shines brightly when you send a gift of love, hope, peace or joy to another. Take a few minutes for reflection.

What has God placed in your heart today that inspires you and brings you joy that you can share with others? Your light will be like a magnet and a vibrational match to another, inspiring them to let their light shine. Begin to share your light and let it shine brightly to illuminate the world with God's love.

Take three deep diaphragmatic breaths. Then, ask God to reveal the light He placed within your heart and ways to let it shine.

Journal your thoughts and express gratitude for the light within your heart that you can share with the world. Reflect on how you can encourage others to let their light shine.

Whispers of Gratitude...What three things are you grateful for today?

_____

_____

_____

Blessings and Love from my Heart to Yours,
Sandy

17 THE POWER OF A PET'S LOVE

Unconditional Love

As humans, we all have one basic need in common...to be loved unconditionally. Ironically, this is one basic need that is sometimes difficult to get from or give to others, especially when you have been hurt, offended or disrespected. Maybe you hurt someone special and they are unable to love you unconditionally. This may happen in a home with family members, friends or loved ones. I believe God created pets to remind and teach us about unconditional love. When you are sad, depressed or frustrated and need your spirits lifted, take time to be with your pet. If you do not have a pet, visit a local animal shelter, pet store or a pet at a friend's home. Notice how your spirits lift as a pet fills your heart with the power of their unconditional love, the greatest power on earth.

Take three deep diaphragmatic breaths and reflect on ways to develop a more loving nature and unconditional love for others. If you would like to surround yourself with love that keeps on giving, local animal shelters are always in need of volunteers. Reach out and share the love.

Journal your thoughts about ways you can begin to express love unconditionally.

Whispers of Gratitude...What three things are you grateful for today?

_____

_____

_____

Blessings and Love from my Heart to Yours,
Sandy

Soul Awakenings

Are there times when your heart whispers and you experience an uncomfortable feeling deep within your belly? This may occur during a certain situation or when you are with a specific person. This is the inner wisdom of your soul, awakening you to the situation at hand. It is like an internal alarm system warning you to pay attention, reminding you to be mindful and aware. This inner wisdom of your soul may prompt you to change your direction, thoughts or something in your life.

Take three deep diaphragmatic breaths whenever you sense this feeling deep within your belly. Mindful breathing will help calm your mind, allowing more clarity about what is happening as your soul awakens. Then, be still and listen to the whispers within your heart and what action, if any, you need to take.

Journal about a time when the inner wisdom of your soul was awakening you to pay attention to a certain situation. What action did you take or could have taken?

Whispers of Gratitude...What three things are you grateful for today?

_____

_____

_____

Blessings and Love from my Heart to Yours,
Sandy

19 THE POWER OF EMOTIONS

Going with the Flow

We have been blessed with emotions to help us understand what we are experiencing in life. Your emotions will tell you when you are going with the flow or against the flow of life. Do you ever feel like you are going against the current in life instead of going with the natural flow? When you go against the flow, life becomes more challenging because you are out of alignment with your Creator and what He has purposed for you to do in the physical realm. When you go against the flow, you are living your life based on your feelings and emotions instead of by faith. You may feel disempowered and may experience feelings of anger, depression, anxiety, frustration, guilt or fear. Going with the flow draws you closer to your Source of life and takes you to higher frequencies such as joy, passion, love and relief.

Take three deep diaphragmatic breaths. Begin to become aware of your feelings and emotions for they will reveal if you are going with or against the flow. As you begin to align with the Source of your life, you will go with the flow instead of letting the power of your emotions take control.

Journal your thoughts. Do you tend to go with or against the flow of life? What one small step can you take to begin to go with the flow?

Whispers of Gratitude...What three things are you grateful for today?

_____

_____

_____

Blessings and Love from my Heart to Yours,
Sandy

20 IT IS YOUR TIME

Heart-Centered Whispers

Do you ever wonder, "Who am I and what am I meant to be doing with the rest of my life?" You may be an empty nester, divorced, changing careers, retired, have lost your spouse or have lost your job. Your life or interests have changed, and now you are unsure of the next step. Have you spent most of your life living up to others' expectations about how to live your life while setting aside your own needs and desires? This will create uncertainty in your mind. My dear heart friend, it is *your time* to experience the longings within your heart. Find a quiet place or go to your sacred healing place for reflection time to listen to the heart-centered whispers within your heart.

Take three deep diaphragmatic breaths and listen to what your heart is telling you. What brings *you* joy and contentment? Practice setting an intention a few minutes each day to listen closely to the heart-centered whispers and longings within *your* heart and soul. As you meditate on your intention, your inner-being or spirit will guide you to the next step.

Journal your thoughts and feelings and what brings *you* joy. Then prepare yourself for a new and exciting journey. IT IS YOUR TIME!

Whispers of Gratitude...What three things are you grateful for today?

_____

_____

_____

Blessings and Love from my Heart to Yours,
Sandy

The Season of Nourishment and Healing

The whispers of summer provide nourishment for our mind, body and soul. The warmth of the morning sun, the musical sounds of birds singing their cheerful songs, the calming sounds of sprinklers nourishing the earth, the serenity of nature, the aromatic smells of flowers and freshly cut grass are all soothing to the soul. Schedule time each day during the summer to embrace and soak in the beauty and healing properties of the season of nourishment and healing.

Take three deep diaphragmatic breaths and give thanks to your Creator for the beautiful gifts of nature during summer wherever you live.

Journal your thoughts about how summer nourishes and heals your mind, body and soul.

Whispers of Gratitude...What three things are you grateful for today?

_____

_____

_____

Blessings and Love from my Heart to Yours,
Sandy

The Source of Your Strength

Do you have days when your heart feels heavy and anxious? There may be days when you feel weighed down by life's challenges and it feels like you are carrying the weight of the world on your shoulders. During these times remember to keep your thoughts on the present moment and centered on God, allowing His peace to calm your anxious heart. Even when you do not understand or feel like it, put your faith and trust in Him for He is your peace.

Take three deep diaphragmatic breaths and feel the calm in your heart as you center your mind on the present moment and the source of your strength.

Journal about what is weighing on your heart today and one step you can take to begin to keep your thoughts centered on the Source of your strength as He calms your anxious heart.

Whispers of Gratitude...What three things are you grateful for today?

_____

_____

_____

Blessings and Love from my Heart to Yours,
Sandy

Take Time for Prayer and Meditation

Taking time to be still, pray and meditate helps to quiet the chatter in our minds, relieves stress and brings us closer to our Creator. There are formal and informal meditations which can be performed anywhere in a few seconds or several hours. Meditation may be mental, visual or physical. A *mindful meditation* focuses on awareness, being conscious of the present moment and is a perfect time to pray and meditate on God's word. A *walking meditation* focuses on your breath and your feet connecting and grounding you to the earth. A *seated meditation* simply quiets your mind while sitting in a chair or on a pillow on the floor. A *body scan meditation* focuses on releasing areas of tension in your body from head to toe. All forms of meditation reduce stress hormones in the body, rebalance energy levels and create calm and restoration.

Take three deep diaphragmatic breaths and begin to focus on your thoughts and feelings

Journal about how you are feeling at this very moment. How are your thoughts affecting your feelings? Are you calm or anxious? Happy or sad? Next, choose a form of meditation to quiet your mind, keep you in the present moment and connect you to your inner being and Creator while refreshing your mind, body and spirit.

Whispers of Gratitude...What three things are you grateful for today?

_____

_____

_____

Blessings and Love from my Heart to Yours,
Sandy

Your Spiritual Destiny

What feeling do you experience when you hear or say the word love? Love is the greatest power on earth and is the destination of your spiritual journey. When you give love away to another, you open the door to receive love back. Words can be encouraging or discouraging and hurtful. Do your words and actions towards others come from love? How others react to you and what you attract to you are good indicators. Whenever we are not coming from love we are disconnected from our Creator, our Source of life, for He is love. Take time today to notice your words when you speak to others. Are your words and actions coming from love?

Anytime you notice your words are not loving and kind, stop and take three deep diaphragmatic breaths. Then, ask God to change your heart so your words and actions come from love, the greatest power on earth.

Journal about how thoughts of love changed your day today.

Whispers of Gratitude...What three things are you grateful for today?

_____

_____

_____

Blessings and Love from my Heart to Yours,
Sandy

Unlimited Choices

Just as the sky is limitless so are possibilities. You have been blessed with infinite possibilities to enjoy each day and live your life to the fullest. Doubts, circumstances or past experiences may prevent you from believing this. Your mind is very powerful and will determine the outcome of your day and life. Negative thoughts result in negative outcomes, and positive thoughts result in positive outcomes. Your intentions determine which path you will choose. Pure and simple. Each day you are presented with unlimited choices. You can choose to wake up dreading the day or choose to wake up embracing the day with open arms, anticipating the infinite possibilities the day will bring. Begin today to recognize your thoughts during the day. Then, set your intention and notice the infinite possibilities that emerge.

Take three deep diaphragmatic breaths and journal your intention for today. Which path will you choose? It is your choice.

Whispers of Gratitude...What three things are you grateful for today?

_____

_____

_____

Blessings and Love from my Heart to Yours,
Sandy

The Source of Your Well-Being

Rainbows remind me of God's promises and eternal love. I envision them as a connection between heaven and earth and the source of our well-being. The colors of the rainbows also remind me of the human body because the colors replicate seven segments within the spinal column. Each segment connects to a specific part of the body through nerve endings. When bodily systems are out of balance, signals are sent to a specific area within your body. The imbalance compromises your physical and emotional health resulting in illness and disease. Meditating and praying on God's promises will help to bring your system back into balance. Practicing mindful movements such as Yoga, Pilates, Tai Chi, and Qi gong along with mindful breathing and aromatherapy will also begin to balance your physical, emotional and spiritual health

Take three deep diaphragmatic breaths and a minute for reflection. Which area(s) of your body feels out of balance? Begin to send health, love and healing thoughts into this area.

Take three more deep breaths and ask the Source of your well-being to reveal areas requiring your attention. Journal these insights and 1-2 steps you can begin today to bring your system back into balance.

Whispers of Gratitude...What three things are you grateful for today?

_____

_____

_____

Blessings and Love from my Heart to Yours,
Sandy

Free Gifts

Have you ever received an unexpected check in the mail, a lead on a new job or you surprisingly forgave someone who hurt you deeply either physically or emotionally? These are whispers of grace and free gifts from our Creator. Sometimes we take these gifts for granted and are unaware of the grace being extended to us. For example, as humans we may not "feel" like forgiving someone. Being able to forgive someone is a gift of God's grace. These unexpected gifts of grace are reminders to help you through difficult times and to give you hope. When we become aware of, receive and accept these gifts, we are then equipped to extend grace to others.

Take three deep diaphragmatic breaths and reflect on a time when you received grace. Does anyone come to mind who may need your forgiveness through God's grace? Could this be you? Do you need to forgive yourself and receive God's grace? Express your gratitude today to the One who extends His amazing grace to us all. My prayer for you today -Thank you God for the sweet sound of your amazing grace. May the person reading this inspiration feel the presence of your love and grace. Amen!

Journal your thoughts on ways you received grace and anyone you have blessed with the gift of God's grace.

Whispers of Gratitude...What three things are you grateful for today?

_____

_____

_____

Blessings and Love from my Heart to Yours,
Sandy

All is Well

Everything you have in your life manifests from your thoughts, words and actions. How you envision your life will be manifested when your thoughts, feelings and actions are in alignment with each other. Everything that happens in your life is perfectly timed. This is the law of nature. One of the hardest things for humans to do is to wait. When you have feelings of doubt, dwell on the past, worry about the future or try to control and make things happen when you think they should, you are not going with the flow of life and are out of alignment with God's plan for your life.

Take three deep diaphragmatic breaths and know that all is well as your life unfolds step by step. Then, wait, know and believe because wonderful things are about to happen!

Take time to journal about something you may be experiencing today and believe and know you are right where you are meant to be. Then, wait to see what unfolds.

Whispers of Gratitude...What three things are you grateful for today?

_____

_____

_____

Blessings and Love from my Heart to Yours,
Sandy

Happiness vs. Joy

Life has taught us to believe things bring us happiness such as a dream home, financial freedom, owning a business, a new car or getting married just to name a few. We may feel unhappy when our day does not go as planned, someone disappoints us or we are unable to afford something we really want. There is a difference between happiness and joy. Happiness is an emotion, is temporary and is based on worldly things. Have you strived to achieve or experience happiness during your lifetime at one time or another and after a while the happiness fades away? Joy, on the other hand, is heart-centered and comes from inside when God is in your heart. It is always there regardless of circumstances, dreams or goals.

Take three deep diaphragmatic breaths as you reflect on times in your life when you experienced happiness. Then, reflect on times when you experienced heart-centered joy.

Capture these thoughts in your journal for insight into what your heart is telling you about happiness vs. joy. How would you describe the difference between happiness and joy?

Whispers of Gratitude...What three things are you grateful for today?

_____

_____

_____

Blessings and Love from my Heart to Yours,
Sandy

Peace Minutes

How much time do you devote to silence each day? Silence is the source of inner peace, and God is the source of our peace according to Mother Teresa. In this fast-paced world, time is limited for moments of silence or to listen to the quiet whispers of your heart. Does your day get so busy that you do not have time to stop and be still or silent? Silence is necessary to refresh your mind, body and spirit. Begin today to intentionally devote time for silence and a minute of peace. Set aside one minute each day for a peace minute.

Take three deep diaphragmatic breaths and begin to experience one minute of peace in silence.

Journal about one promise you can make to yourself each day for a "peace minute" to refresh your mind, body and spirit.

Whispers of Gratitude...What three things are you grateful for today?

_____

_____

_____

Blessings and Love from my Heart to Yours,
Sandy

31 AN EVENING MEDITATION

Tranquil Moments

Are there times when you feel like you are burning the candle at both ends leaving you feeling exhausted by the end of the day? Relaxing after a busy day and getting a restful night's sleep of at least 7-8 hours is important to balance your energy, renew your mind and refresh your soul. Set aside a few minutes each night for tranquil moments with an evening meditation prior to going to bed. Begin by creating your own personal sacred healing space.

Take three deep diaphragmatic breaths. Continue to focus on your breath, then, breathe in 4 counts, pause 2 counts, breathe out 4 counts and pause 2 counts. Repeat 2 more times. Enhance your meditation and quiet time by listening to relaxing music, enjoying a cup of hot tea and diffusing or inhaling your favorite essential oil.

Take time to journal about your meditation experience and embrace the tranquility of the moment. Finish your day with a soothing and relaxing warm bath or foot soak using your favorite essential oil. Ahhh... enjoy the calm and tranquil moments. You are worth it!

Whispers of Gratitude...What three things are you grateful for today?

_____

_____

_____

Blessings and Love from my Heart to Yours,
Sandy

Inner Beauty

Time is perpetual and continues to move forward as nature takes its course. Each breath we take is a gift from our Creator, each wrinkle is a memory in our life and each gray hair has brought wisdom. Beauty comes from deep within our hearts. How we perceive the aging process is a matter of our feelings and beliefs. Our minds have been programmed to feel our age. Instead, age gracefully by choosing to feel *young, vibrant* and *alive* regardless of your age. You have been created from love and are purposed to share your gifts and knowledge with others while you are on this earth. The longer you are on this earth, the more wisdom you will gain preparing you to teach others the lessons you have learned from your life experiences.

Take three deep diaphragmatic breaths. Be thankful for another day and embrace your inner beauty and the elegance of your physical being, for you have been blessed with another day to share your life and wisdom on earth with others.

Journal your thoughts about what you have learned today about your inner beauty and wisdom.

Whispers of Gratitude...What three things are you grateful for today?

Blessings and Love from my Heart to Yours,
Sandy

.

33 REPRESSED EMOTIONS

Creating a Healthy Mind

Repressed emotions affect your emotional, physical and spiritual health. Circumstances throughout life may leave scars and bad memories resulting in anxiety, depression, fear, anger or resentment all affecting your health. Always remember you have been made in God's image and were created with a healthy mind, body and spirit.

Take a few minutes for three deep diaphragmatic breaths. Then, ask God to reveal any repressed emotions you may have deep within your heart and ask Him to change your thoughts about the situation to support the healing process. Diffuse or inhale your favorite essential oil to calm your mind and promote emotional healing.

Journal your thoughts about memories that arise and how you can begin to create a healthy mind to heal from any repressed emotions.

Whispers of Gratitude...What three things are you grateful for today?

_____

_____

_____

_____

Blessings and Love from my Heart to Yours,
Sandy

The Winds of Grace During Harvest Time

Fall is a season for change. The trees shed their summer leaves as the winds begin to blow. When you hear the winds blowing during the whispers of fall, imagine experiencing supernatural grace empowering you to do things you are meant to do. Obstacles will be overcome, and the true desires and dreams in your heart will begin to turn into reality as you experience the gentle winds of grace during harvest time. The right opportunities and the right people will miraculously begin to appear reminding you of God's grace.

Take three deep diaphragmatic breaths as you open your heart and listen to the sweet sounds of the winds. Imagine and feel God's grace flowing through your entire being.

Take time for reflection and journal your thoughts about how the winds of grace changed your life over the years.

Whispers of Gratitude...What three things are you grateful for today?

_____

_____

_____

_____

Blessings and Love from my Heart to Yours,
Sandy

Agents Undercover

Has anyone ever come into your life unexpectedly who helped you overcome adversities? Maybe you were struggling financially or needed emotional support. Maybe you had to make a business decision or a career change and someone came into your life who guided you towards the next step and then, sometimes they were never to be seen again. This has happened to me several times over the years. People have shown up in my life providing exactly what I needed at the time such as an encouraging word, financial help or a book to read, guiding me to the next step in my life. I never saw some of them again. I believe these are undercover agents sent by God. He sends human angels to protect us, guide us and keep us from harm as a reminder of His never-ending love.

Take three deep diaphragmatic breaths and ask God to send His angels to you. They are patiently waiting to carry out God's plans for your life. Remember, you too, my friend, have been, are or will be an undercover agent and human angel on earth for someone else.

Reflect and journal about a time when you needed supernatural help and God blessed you by sending a human angel on earth.

Whispers of Gratitude...What three things are you grateful for today?

_____

_____

_____

Blessings and Love from my Heart to Yours,
Sandy

Heart-Centered Living

You have been blessed with special gifts and talents to share with the world through your work life. The world has evolved over the years and the use of technology allows you to reach multitudes of people. Working from your home or starting a home-based business presents the opportunity for a work/life balance. When the work you do is heart-centered, you will experience boundless joy as you share your gifts and talents with others. What are you passionate about? Do you lose track of time while doing certain things? Does the type of work you do bring joy to your heart? These are indications that you are doing what you love to do.

Take three deep diaphragmatic breaths and a few moments to prepare your heart. Then, listen to the quiet whispers God placed in your heart. Are you comfortable and joyful where you are at or do you need to consider making some changes?

Journal your thoughts about what brings joy to your heart and then begin your journey to heart-centered living and doing the work you love.

Whispers of Gratitude...What three things are you grateful for today?

_____

_____

_____

Blessings and Love from my Heart to Yours,
Sandy

37 LOVE AND RELATIONSHIPS

Lift Your Frequencies Higher

Relationships can be challenging at times which makes it hard to extend love to another person. Have you ever been offended by someone close to you? People may say something offensive to you either intentionally or unintentionally that affect your emotions. You do not have control over their actions or words. However, you do have control over how you respond.

The next time this happens to you, take three deep diaphragmatic breaths. Then, make a conscious choice to move from the physical realm to the spiritual realm by shifting your thoughts to a higher frequency of love. You have been created from love, so choose to lift your frequencies higher to love sending love to the other person. Notice how the situation or your feelings about this person begin to change.

Journal your thoughts about how you can shift your thoughts to a higher frequency of love or about a time when you made this shift. What was the outcome?

Whispers of Gratitude...What three things are you grateful for today?

_____

_____

_____

Blessings and Love from my Heart to Yours,
Sandy

Mindful and Centered Breathing

Life comes from each breath you take. Oxygen is necessary to sustain life. Without oxygen, you would cease to exist on earth. When you were born, your breath began within your diaphragm. If you watch a baby breathe, you will notice the baby's belly going up and down with each breath. As we go through life, this breathing pattern is altered due to stress and anxiety in our lives resulting in shallow breathing from the chest instead of deep within the diaphragm. Shallow breaths prevent your body from getting the oxygen it needs to function efficiently resulting in imbalances. Negative stress also alters your breathing pattern causing your body to develop different breathing patterns to cope with unpleasant situations. Begin this moment to practice mindful and centered breathing to re-balance your body and energy.

Take three deep diaphragmatic mindful breaths, noticing each inhalation as it enters your body and each exhalation as it exits your body. As you follow the flow of your breath, notice the coolness of the air as you inhale and the warmth of the air as you exhale. Take time each day to balance your energy by practicing mindful and centered breathing – your life force.

Journal about how you feel when you practice mindful and centered breathing and JUST B-R-E-A-T-H-E!

Whispers of Gratitude...What three things are you grateful for today?

_____

_____

_____

Blessings and Love from my Heart to Yours,
Sandy

.

Courageous Hearts of Women

Fear can prevent you from listening to the whispers within your heart. You may fear change itself, disapproval of others, failure or success. Fear may result in anxiety and self-sabotaging behaviors, preventing you from manifesting your dreams. Remember, you are a child of God who loves and values you above all others. He placed dreams within your heart and will give you the strength and courage to make them come alive. Does fear prevent you from moving toward your dreams? Set an intention to ignore the inner critic inside of you causing self-doubt and apprehension. Whenever fear begins to take hold, create a quiet place either virtually or physically and ask God to reveal what is causing the fear in your heart. Ask Him for the confidence and courage you need to manifest your dreams and live the life He designed specifically for you.

Take three deep diaphragmatic breaths and pray for wisdom, strength and a courageous heart to take the actions necessary to overcome your fears. Be strong and take faith-based action as you develop a courageous heart.

Journal about the dreams God placed within your heart and the fears He has revealed to you. Then, trust Him for the strength and courage to move towards your dreams.

Whispers of Gratitude...What three things are you grateful for today?

_____

_____

_____

Blessings and Love from my Heart to Yours,
Sandy

Give Thanks

As days present challenges, our natural tendency may be to think negative thoughts. Thanksgiving Day is a perfect time to begin to change your thoughts to express gratitude for your life experiences and give thanks even when you do not "feel" like it. Expressing a heart of gratitude brings feelings of joy into your life and the lives of those you care about. Gratitude cancels out negative thoughts. Life gives us back what we project outward. The next time you notice your attitude is negative *choose* to change your thoughts to an *attitude of gratitude*. Thanksgiving Day is also a perfect time to express your gratitude and love for others as you gather together. My prayer of gratitude to you - I am so very grateful for the opportunity to share these inspirations with you, the love of family, friends and God's love and grace. Amen!

Take three deep diaphragmatic breaths and reflect on all the things you are grateful for and give thanks with a grateful heart.

Journal your thoughts about ways you can begin to express a heart of gratitude.

Whispers of Gratitude...What three things are you grateful for today?

_____

_____

_____

Blessings and Love from my Heart to Yours,
Sandy

Walk in the Light

Every day you have a choice to walk in the light or walk in darkness. When you begin to make conscious choices and open your heart to the light, the dark shadows in your life will begin to disappear. Light shadows will begin to dominate your thoughts, drawing you closer to the light, overcoming the shadows of darkness such as jealousy, anger, addictions, judgment or a controlling nature. To heal and move from the dark to the light, ask God to reveal the dark shadows in your life and change your heart so you can begin to walk in the light for *He is the light*. This will require courage, honesty and compassion towards yourself as you consciously become aware of something that may have caused harm or hurt to yourself or another.

Take three deep diaphragmatic breaths and a few moments to acknowledge any dark shadows that may be keeping you from the light.

Journal your thoughts about one way you can begin to overcome shadows of darkness by walking in the light.

Whispers of Gratitude...What three things are you grateful for today?

_____

_____

_____

Blessings and Love from my Heart to Yours,
Sandy

Nourishment for your Inner Being

Are there times when your life feels out of balance? During these times you may experience feelings of exhaustion, confusion, anxiety, depression or uncertainty of the purpose and meaning of your life. Your heart, mind or soul will let you know when this happens. Just like our bodies need healthy nourishment, exercise and rest to function, our inner beings also need nourishment. I like to think of this as soul food. Daily prayer and meditation are excellent sources of soul food. When we are connected to our Creator, our inner being is the source of our strength, wisdom, peace of mind, innate health and inspiration. Are you feeling connected or disconnected from your inner being? Do you need to take more time for spiritual self-care or spend more time with the Source of your life?

Take three deep diaphragmatic breaths to bring awareness to your feelings and where your life feels out of balance. Does your inner being need soul food?

Journal about your thoughts and feelings as you ask God for wisdom about ways to nourish your inner being.

Whispers of Gratitude...What three things are you grateful for today?

_____

_____

_____

Blessings and Love from my Heart to Yours,
Sandy

43 A MORNING MEDITATION

Embrace Life

When you awake in the morning, you have been blessed with another opportunity to embrace life. How will you spend your day today? Your thoughts and intentions will determine which course your life will take.

Begin each day with a morning prayer and meditation session to fill your day with joy and positive thoughts. As your day begins, *choose* to look at the *blessing* in each occurrence. Aromatherapy will enhance your morning experience and prepare you for a day full of blessings. Diffuse or inhale your favorite essential oil during your prayer and meditation time.

Take three deep diaphragmatic breaths to quiet your mind as you set your intention for the day. Take a few more mindful breaths. If thoughts arise, acknowledge them, then imagine them floating away like the clouds in the sky as you gently bring your focus back to your breath to stay in the present moment.

Journal about any re-occurring thoughts that arise during your morning session. Are they positive thoughts? If not, embrace life by setting your intention to look at these thoughts as blessings and opportunities for growth.

Whispers of Gratitude...What three things are you grateful for today?

_____

_____

_____

Blessings and Love from my Heart to Yours,
Sandy

A Time for Restoration and Reflection

Winter is a season and time for restoration and reflection. It's a time to reflect on the past year and begin to focus on your direction in life for the new year. Winter is a time to discover and experience stillness in the hectic pace of life as you replenish your energy. It is also a time to enjoy the beauty of nature such as the gentle snowflakes falling from the sky, snow-covered trees and rooftops, the beautiful glow and warmth from a fireplace or the sun, a mesmerizing sunset or the smell of cookies baking in the oven. Are there different choices you wish you had made during the past year or are there things you would like to change in your life for the upcoming year? Would you like to schedule more time for self-care for your physical, emotional and spiritual health? Is it time to reconnect with friends you have not seen in a while?

Create a quiet sacred place and take three deep diaphragmatic breaths to calm your mind and spirit. Then, listen to the quiet whispers of your heart for guidance toward your next journey into the new year.

Journal your thoughts as you reflect upon the whispers of winter and how this inspiration inspired you to make any changes in your life for the new year.

Whispers of Gratitude...What three things are you grateful for today?

_____

_____

_____

Blessings and Love from my Heart to Yours,
Sandy

45 THE POWER OF INTENTION

Be Mindful of Your Thoughts

Our words and actions begin with a thought and an intention. Intentions may be conscious or subconscious, positive or negative and are very powerful. Actions always begin with an intention and intentions always begin with a thought. Have you ever said something to someone and later regretted your words and actions? Becoming conscious and mindfully aware of your thoughts may prevent you from doing or saying something you will regret later.

Take three deep diaphragmatic breaths to become mindful of your thoughts and to identify if your thoughts are coming from your heart. Will your words help and encourage another or be hurtful? By consciously awakening to each moment and identifying your intention, you will begin to make choices that change how you relate to others. Begin today to be mindful of your thoughts and your intentions when you interact with another.

Journal about any changes that are necessary for you to become more mindful of your thoughts and your intentions.

Whispers of Gratitude...What three things are you grateful for today?

_____

_____

_____

Blessings and Love from my Heart to Yours,
Sandy

.

Three Simple Steps

Are there times when you have asked for something, and nothing transpired or at least not the way you expected? Maybe you lost or left your job, needed financial help or you were asking for a change in your attitude and nothing changed. There are three steps to receiving what we ask for. The first step is to ask. The second step is to believe a change will occur. Sometimes we may unconsciously resist and block the change from happening by thinking negative thoughts. The third step is to be open to receiving and allowing the outcome to transpire no matter what. It is important to let go of your expectations and allow God to take control.

Take three deep diaphragmatic breaths and reflect on what you would like to ask for in the present moment, believe it will happen and then receive the outcome with an open heart and mind.

Journal your thoughts as you ask, believe and receive trusting God is in control.

Whispers of Gratitude...What three things are you grateful for today?

_____

_____

_____

Blessings and Love from my Heart to Yours,
Sandy

The Gifts of Three Wise Men

Christmas is a wonderful time of year to enjoy time with loved ones to exchange gifts and share a meal together. It is also easy to get caught up in the hustle and bustle during this time of year and forget the true meaning of Christmas, the birth of Jesus. It is a time of year to not only receive gifts but to give back to our Creator. The Three Wise Men gave gifts of Gold, Frankincense and Myrrh to the baby Jesus.

Take three deep diaphragmatic breaths and set aside a few minutes of silence to reflect on the true meaning of Christmas.

Journal your thoughts about the gift(s) you will give back to the One who loves you with an everlasting love, who gave His all and is the Source of your life.

Whispers of Gratitude...What three things are you grateful for today?

_____

_____

_____

Blessings and Love from my Heart to Yours,
Sandy

A One Minute Prayer and Meditation

Prepare to listen to the quiet whispers God places upon your heart for spiritual healing by taking three deep diaphragmatic breaths.

Father, thank you for your unconditional love. Thank you for the gifts you have given me and for allowing me to be a light in the world. Teach me how to share my gifts with others. Grant me the courage to express these gifts, especially during times when I feel inadequate and worthless. Wash away anything that may stand in the way of expressing my gifts. Teach me how to make wise choices and to forgive myself for any past choices I have made that have not served you. Help me to walk by faith and to believe I have a purpose and destiny. Show me how to be a light so others may see your unconditional love through me. Amen!

Take three deep diaphragmatic breaths and journal your thoughts about how God is teaching you ways to strengthen your spiritual health.

Whispers of Gratitude...What three things are you grateful for today?

_____

_____

_____

Blessings and Love from my Heart to Yours,
Sandy

49 FINANCIAL HEALING

A One Minute Prayer and Meditation

Prepare to listen to the quiet whispers God places upon your heart for financial healing by taking three deep diaphragmatic breaths.

Creator and Master of my life, I have made poor choices with my financial situations, creating anxiety and stress in my life. I feel out of control as my debts keep increasing. My heart is open as I pray for your wisdom, courage and strength to make better decisions about my finances. Help me to practice self-control with my spending habits. I long to help others who are also struggling financially and get discouraged when I am unable to do so because of my financial burdens. Open my eyes to creative ways to pay off my debts so I may help others in need. I am so thankful for your faithfulness as you provide for my daily needs of food, clothing and shelter. I believe in miracles and I am praying for a miracle with my finances. You are a God of abundance. Make me an instrument of your abundance. Amen!

Take three deep diaphragmatic breaths and journal a few thoughts about how God is teaching you ways to strengthen your financial health.

Whispers of Gratitude...What three things are you grateful for today?

_____

_____

_____

Blessings and Love from my Heart to Yours,
Sandy

A One Minute Prayer and Meditation

Prepare to listen to the quiet whispers God places upon your heart for relational healing by taking three deep diaphragmatic breaths.

Lord, help me to open my heart to extend thoughts of love to myself and others every day. Let your light shine brightly through me to those open to receive. Teach me how to express my love through service to others and to greet each day with love in my heart. Loving myself and others can sometimes be challenging. Today, by your grace, I choose to love completely and unconditionally. Thank you for washing away unhealthy thoughts and behaviors. Thank you for the courage to walk away from unhealthy relationships and live a new life filled with love and forgiveness. Teach me how to forgive myself and others by the power of your Holy Spirit for I know forgiveness is not possible in my own strength. Amen!

Take three deep diaphragmatic breaths and journal your thoughts about how God is teaching you ways to strengthen your relational health.

Whispers of Gratitude...What three things are you grateful for today?

_____

_____

_____

Blessings and Love from my Heart to Yours,
Sandy

A One Minute Prayer and Meditation

Prepare to listen to the quiet whispers God places upon your heart for emotional healing by taking three deep diaphragmatic breaths.

Father, I am thankful for the emotions you have given me, allowing me to express myself. Give me the courage and wisdom to be more like you – abounding in love, slow to anger, practicing forgiveness and being filled with inner peace. Grant me the grace to think, speak and act appropriately. Transform me by your healing power to have healthy emotions. Reveal any self-sabotaging behaviors. Help me set healthy boundaries and find joy once again in the things I love such as listening to music, reading, walking in nature, calling a friend, enjoying a hobby or learning a new skill. Fill my heart with an attitude of gratitude as you remind me of things to be grateful for each day. Amen!

Take three deep diaphragmatic breaths and journal your thoughts about ways God is teaching you to strengthen your emotional health.

Whispers of Gratitude...What three things are you grateful for today?

_____

_____

_____

Blessings and Love from my Heart to Yours,
Sandy

A One Minute Prayer and Meditation

Prepare to listen to the quiet whispers God places upon your heart for physical healing by taking three deep diaphragmatic breaths.

Father, I am so thankful for my health and ask for your power to sustain me as I learn to practice self-control and take care of my physical health. Help me to make wise choices to keep my mind, body and spirit healthy. Guide me to take responsibility for the food choices I make, to eat healthy foods, drink enough quality water, incorporate movement into my daily life and eat mindfully. Help me to find relief from stress and anxiety and value myself enough to make time to exercise, rest and enjoy relaxation. Help me to let go of negative or obsessive thoughts such as weighing myself every day or exercising excessively to the point of exhaustion. Teach me how to maintain a healthy balance. Today I will begin to have a positive attitude and take care of my physical health. Amen!

Take three deep diaphragmatic breaths and journal thoughts about ways God is teaching you to strengthen and balance your physical health.

Whispers of Gratitude...What three things are you grateful for today?

_____

_____

_____

Blessings and Love from my Heart to Yours,
Sandy

Sandy Philbin

Sandy Philbin, MA, women's restorative health educator, author and speaker, educates and coaches women to restore their lives by practicing self-love and self-care. She is passionate about teaching health and wellness for the mind, body and spirit. This book was Spirit-inspired and evolved from personal experiences. Sandy is an ACE® Certified Personal Trainer and a licensed CHEK professional. She lives in Spokane, Washington with her husband, Barry and their Red Heeler Mix, Shaylah Belle, a rescue dog. Sandy, Barry and Shaylah have fun staying healthy by walking and doing Pilates together. They participate in fundraisers to support local animal shelters. Connect with Sandy at www.sandyphilbin.com or @sandyphilbin.

INSPIRATIONAL RESOURCES

One-Minute Mindfulness: 50 simple ways to find peace, clarity, and new possibilities in a stressed-out world - Donald Altman

Instant Expert Blueprint: Online Course – Maria Andros-Buckley

Sanity Secrets for Stressed-Out Women: Energize and Renew Your Life - Sue Augustine

Simple Retreats for a Woman's Soul - Sue Augustine

The Solution A 5-Day Emotional Makeover for Controlling Stress and Worry – Lucinda Bassett

The Extraordinary Workplace: Replacing Fear with Trust and Compassion - Danna Beal

Four Year Career Plan: Young Living Edition - Richard Bliss

Inner Peace for Busy Women: Balancing Work, Family, and Your Inner Life - Joan Z. Borysenko, Ph.D.

Pathway to Purpose™ for women: Connecting your to-do list, your passions, and God's purposes for your life – Katie Brazelton

Praying for Purpose for Women: a Prayer experience that will change your life forever - Katie Brazelton

The Motivation Manifesto: 9 Declarations to Claim Your Personal Power - Brendon Burchard

The Secret - Rhonda Byrne

How to Eat, Move and Be Healthy: Your personalized 4-step guide to looking and feeling great from the inside out – Paul Chek

Prayer Therapy: Stop Hurting! – Dr. Minnie Claiborne

The Alchemist - Paulo Coelho

Love and Respect: The Love She Most Desires; The Respect He Desperately Needs - Dr. Emerson Eggerichs

Courage - Debbie Ford

One Minute Inspirations for Women - Elizabeth George

You're Made for a God-Sized Dream – Opening the Door to All God Has for You - Holley Gerth

You Asked God for What?! - Pat Gilliss

Fat Flush Plan - Ann Louise Gittleman

Angels: God's Secret Agents - Billy Graham

Gameplan: The Complete Strategy Guide to go from Starter Kit to Silver - Sarah Harnisch

The Astonishing Power of Emotions: Let Your Feelings Be Your Guide - Jerry and Esther Hicks

Holy Ambition: What It Takes To Make A Difference For God - Chip Ingram

Power Prayers for Women - Jackie M. Johnson

The Millionaire Maker: Act, Think, and Make Money the Way the Wealthy Do - Loral Langemeier

Think and Grow Rich for Women: Using Your Power To Create Success And Significance - Sharon Lechter

The Difference Maker: Making Your Attitude Your Greatest Asset-John C. Maxwell

With God All Things Are Possible: A Handbook of Life-From the Life Study Fellowship

Heal Your Mind, Rewire Your Brain: Applying the Exciting New Science of Brain Synchrony for Creativity, Peace and Presence - Patt Lind-Kyle

The Greatest Success in the World – Og Mandino

40 Days: Inspiration & Encouragement to Get You Through Tough Times – Therese Marszalek

The Power of Simple Prayer: How to Talk with God about Everything – Joyce Meyer

Anatomy of the Spirit: The Seven Stages of Power and Healing - Carolyn Myss, Ph.D.

Your Best Life Now: 90 DEVOTIONS for Living at Your Full Potential – Joel Osteen

Just Enough Light for the Step I'm On: Trusting God in the Tough Times - Stormie Omartian

Take Time for Your Life: A Personal Coach's 7-Step Program for Creating the Life You Want - Cheryl Richardson

Heal Your Mind: Your Prescription for Wholeness through Medicine, Affirmations, and Intuition - Mona Lisa Schulz, M.D., Ph.D., with Louise Hay

Going Beyond Self Sabotage Online Course - J.P. Sears

Meditations for Women Who Do Too Much - Anne Wilson Schaef

Simplify Your Life: Ways to Change the Way You Work So You Have More Time to Live - Elaine St. James

Enter His Gates: A Daily Devotional - Charles Stanley

Daily OM: Inspirational Thoughts for a Happy, Healthy, and Fulfilling Day - Madisyn Taylor
Living Life on Purpose: Discovering God's Best For Your Life - Lysa TerKeurst
Life Application Study Bible NIV: Tyndale House Publishers, Inc. and Zondervan Publishing House

May Your Life Be Blessed With Abundance, Health and New Beginnings.

Love,
Sandy

Made in the USA
Lexington, KY
29 September 2019